Alamo

Steve Goldsworthy

LET'S READ AV² BY WEIGL™
ADDED VALUE • AUDIO VISUAL

Go to **www.av2books.com**, and enter this book's unique code.

BOOK CODE

E 1 6 9 6 8 0

AV² by Weigl brings you media enhanced books that support active learning.

AV² provides enriched content that supplements and complements this book. Weigl's AV² books strive to create inspired learning and engage young minds in a total learning experience.

Your AV² Media Enhanced books come alive with...

Audio
Listen to sections of the book read aloud.

Video
Watch informative video clips.

Embedded Weblinks
Gain additional information for research.

Try This!
Complete activities and hands-on experiments.

Key Words
Study vocabulary, and complete a matching word activity.

Quizzes
Test your knowledge.

Slide Show
View images and captions, and prepare a presentation.

... and much, much more!

Published by AV² by Weigl
350 5th Avenue, 59th Floor, New York, NY 10118
Website: www.av2books.com   www.weigl.com

Library of Congress Control Number: 2012940120

ISBN 978-1-61913-080-7 (hard cover)
ISBN 978-1-61913-299-3 (soft cover)

Printed in the United States of America in North Mankato, Minnesota
1 2 3 4 5 6 7 8 9 16 15 14 13 12

052012
WEP050412

Editor: Aaron Carr   **Design:** Mandy Christiansen

Photo Credits
Every reasonable effort has been made to trace ownership and to obtain permission to reprint copyright material. The publishers would be pleased to have any errors or omissions brought to their attention so that they may be corrected in subsequent printings.

Weigl acknowledges Getty Images as the primary image supplier for this title.

CONTENTS

What is the Alamo?

The Alamo was the place of an important battle.
The battle was fought between Mexico and Texas.

5

BONHAM

BOWI

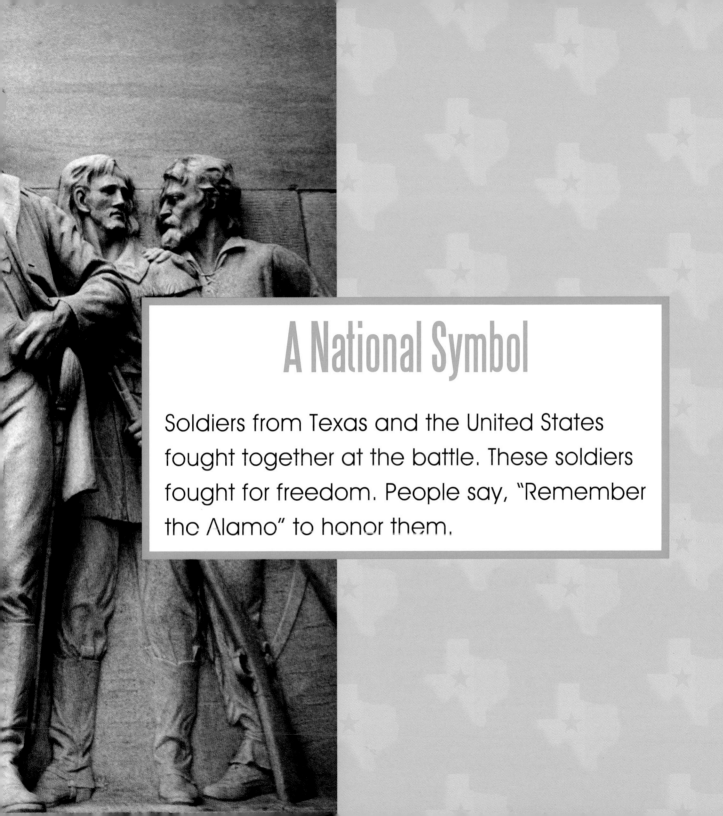

A National Symbol

Soldiers from Texas and the United States fought together at the battle. These soldiers fought for freedom. People say, "Remember the Alamo" to honor them.

How did the Alamo get its Name?

The Alamo was named after a tree that grows in Texas. The tree is called the *álamo,*

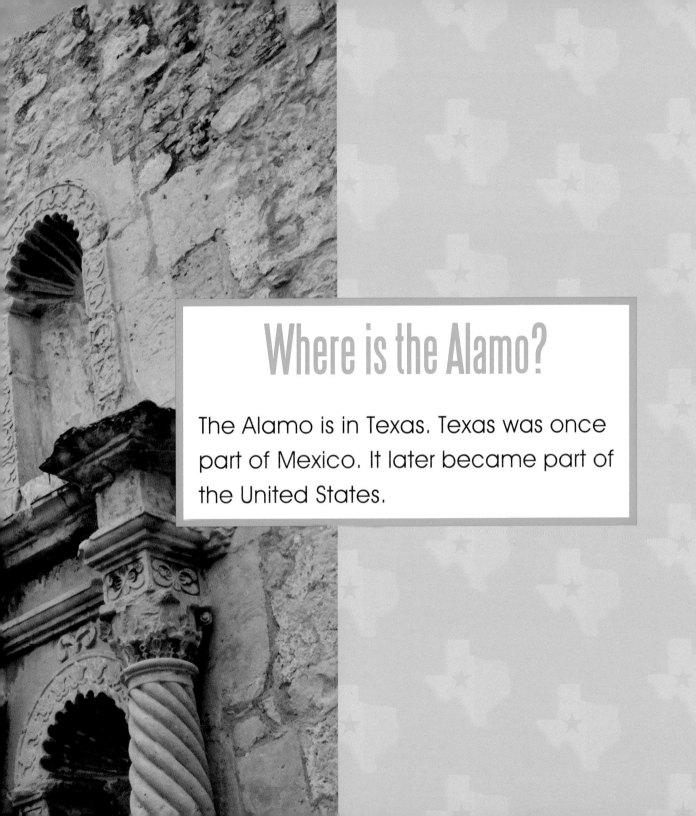

Where is the Alamo?

The Alamo is in Texas. Texas was once part of Mexico. It later became part of the United States.

Why was the Alamo Built?

The Alamo was built to be a mission. A mission is a place that has a small church and houses where priests live.

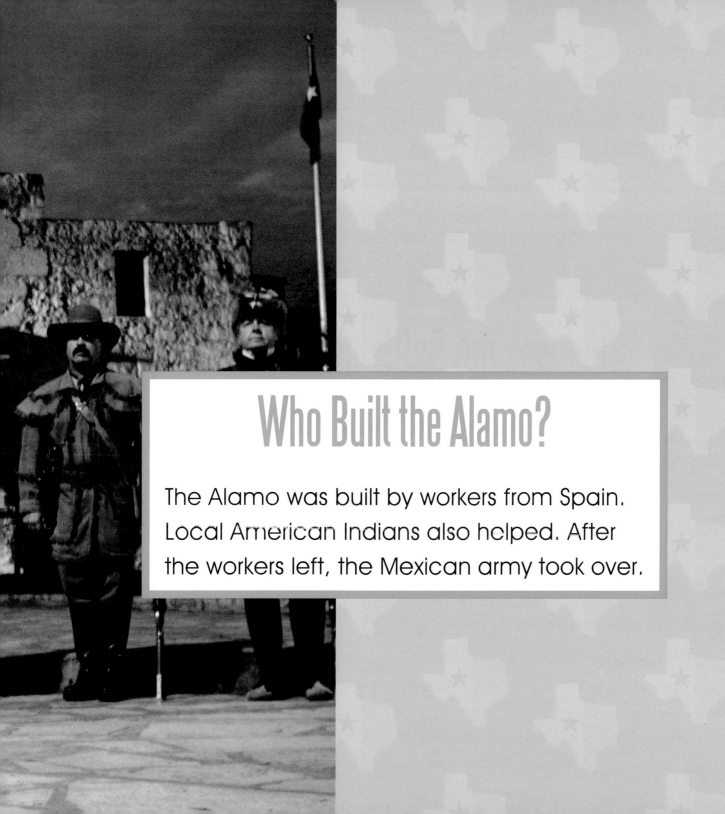

Who Built the Alamo?

The Alamo was built by workers from Spain. Local American Indians also helped. After the workers left, the Mexican army took over.

What was the Battle of the Alamo?

The Battle of the Alamo was fought for the freedom of Texas. The battle went on for 13 days.

Who were the Famous People at the Battle of Alamo?

Some famous people fought in the Battle of the Alamo. One of them was Davy Crockett. He is a famous folk hero.

The Alamo Today

More than two million people visit the Alamo each year. The Alamo has three museums. These museums tell the history of the Alamo and Texas.

ALAMO FACTS

These pages provide detailed information that expands on the interesting facts found in the book. These pages are intended to be used by adults as a learning support to help young readers round out their knowledge of each national symbol featured in the *American Icons* series.

Pages 4–5

What is the Alamo? The Alamo was the location of an important battle during the Texas Revolution. This was a war fought between Mexico and settlers of Texas. In 1835, new laws in Mexico led American and Mexican residents of Texas to seek independence. On March 6, 1836, Mexican troops attacked and took over the Alamo. Texas won the war on April 21.

Pages 6–7

A National Symbol The Alamo is the most famous tourist site in Texas. It is a symbol of bravery for many Americans. After the battle of the Alamo, many Texans and Americans were inspired to join the fight. During the final battle of the Texas Revolution, U.S. Army soldiers shouted, "Remember the Alamo!" The Alamo is also a place to honor the people who died there.

Pages 8–9

How did the Alamo get its Name? The exact inspiration for the name of the Alamo is not known. It may have been named after a local cottonwood tree called the *álamo*. The Alamo was first occupied by Spanish soldiers from Álamo de Parras in the Mexican state of Coahuila. Their nickname, the "Alamo Company," may also have inspired the name.

Pages 10–11

Where is the Alamo? The Alamo stands in what is now the U.S. city of San Antonio, Texas. At the time of the Texas Revolution, this land was in Mexico, and the town was called San Fernando de Béxar. In 1836, Texas defeated Mexico in the Texas Revolution and became an independent republic. In 1845, Texas joined the United States as the 28th state.

Why was the Alamo Built? The Alamo was built as a religious mission in the early 1700s. The original complex was made up of several buildings, including a chapel, a stone residence for priests, barracks for the American Indians living and working at the mission, and a textiles workshop. By the early 1800s, the mission was abandoned. The Mexican military took control of the site.

Who Built the Alamo? Over several years, Spanish workers and local American Indian workers built a number of structures at the site of the Alamo. At first, these buildings were made of mud and straw. Later buildings were made of wood and stone. When the Mexican military took over the complex, they added stone arches, ramps, and a palisade for defense.

What was the Battle of the Alamo? On February 23, 1836, more than 1,500 Mexican troops arrived at San Fernando de Béxar in an attempt to regain control of Texas. Mexican soldiers attacked the Alamo. The Texans fended off the attack. Then, on March 6, Mexican soldiers stormed the Alamo, climbing the walls and overwhelming the defenders. More than 180 Texans died, and about 600 Mexican soldiers were killed or wounded.

Who were the Famous People at the Battle of the Alamo? Three people became well-known folk heroes after the Battle of the Alamo. At the time of the battle, Colonel James Bowie and Cavalry Officer William B. Travis were co-commanders of the Alamo troops. Politician, soldier, and frontiersman Davy Crockett joined them on February 8. All three died in the March 6 attack.

The Alamo Today More than 2 million people visit the Alamo each year. The complex consists of three main buildings. The main chapel has been renamed the Shrine. There is also the Long Barrack Museum and the Gift Museum. These buildings house artifacts related to the history of the Texas Revolution and the history of Texas.

Key Words

Research has shown that as much as 65 percent of all written material published in English is made up of 300 words. These 300 words cannot be taught using pictures or learned by sounding them out. They must be recognized by sight. This book contains 63 common sight words to help young readers improve their reading fluency and comprehension. This book also teaches young readers several important content words, such as nouns. These words are paired with pictures to aid in learning and improve understanding.

Page	Sight Words First Appearance
4	an, and, between, important, is, of, place, the, was, what
7	a, at, for, from, people, say, them, these, to, together
8	after, did, get, grows, how, in, its, name, that, tree
11	it, later, once, part, where
12	be, has, houses, live, small, why
15	also, American, by, Indians, left, over, took, who
16	days, on, went
19	he, one, some, were
21	each, more, tell, than, three, two, year

Page	Content Words First Appearance
4	Alamo, battle, Mexico, Texas
7	freedom, soldiers, symbol, United States
8	álamo
12	church, mission, priests
15	army, Spain, workers
16	freedom
19	Davy Crockett, folk hero
21	history, museums

Check out www.av2books.com for activities, videos, audio clips, and more!

1 Go to www.av2books.com.

2 Enter book code. | E 1 6 9 6 8 0 |

3 Fuel your imagination online!

www.av2books.com